HARRY CHARNOCK'S
MOTORING VERSE

My late father, W.H. Charnock, better known as Harry Charnock, was born in 1902. He was educated at Lancing and St John's College Cambridge, where he graduated with a degree in Civil Engineering and joined the London North Eastern Railway. At the outbreak of war he enlisted with the Royal Engineers but due to ill health was unable to serve abroad. In 1943 he was invalided out of the Army and rejoined the LNER until the end of hostilities when he and my mother retired to West Sussex.

My father had many, to me, exhausting interests including very competitive cross country running at school and serious potholing and pioneering cave exploration at University and afterwards. This was followed by cross country motorcycling in later years. On retirement he was heavily involved in resurrecting the Bentley Drivers Club after the war and served on the Committee. He also devoted his time to painting and writing both serious and light hearted verse, together with fettling and occasionally competing with his collection of rather tired motor cars. These included two W.O. $4\frac{1}{2}$ litre Bentleys. 105 Airline Talbot, Alvis Silver Eagle Special and a much loved family Rover Speed 14, together with a Triumph twin motor cycle. He died in 1959.

Tony Charnock

Born of ancient Peak District family, dating to at least the 13th century and complete with the Eyam Gene and an escutcheon, whatever that is. Complicated admixture of Romany and erudite blood turned feet to Bohemia rather than family tendency to scholarship. Reared by headmaster grandfather—bottom still sore. Became circus aerialist. Fell. Stopped doing it. Went into music hall/variety. Death of same. Went to art school; often. Exhibited paintings and self at outdoor art shows. Discovered by Advertising Profession. Became commercial artist, photographer, motoring journalist, cabaret performer and many other things, not necessarily in that order. Interested in cooking, wine, women, some other people, and laughter.

Red Daniells

Harry Charnock's
Motoring Verse

DRUMHOUSE LTD

2002

The majority of these poems were
originally published in 1959 by
Villiers Publications Ltd,
Ingestre Road, London NW5

ISBN 1-899743-02-2

Published in 2002 by
Drumhouse Ltd
Pitfour
Kington
Herefordshire
HR5 3BB

01544 231133

Printed by Quorum Technical Services Ltd,
Cheltenham, Gloucestershire, GL51 8PL

PUBLISHER'S FOREWORD

Harry Charnock has always been a cult figure in the world of elderly motors. We look upon him as our Poet Laureate.

This edition has been enlarged by a number of poems that were not included in the original anthology. We have embellished the book with some wonderful pen and ink drawings by Red Daniells.

Let us hope that Harry Charnock's poems will entertain a new generation of enthusiasts and introduce them to the Golden Days of Motoring.

We are indebted to Tony Charnock and his family for their consent and cooperation in producing this book.

Roger Collings
President VSCC 1986–1990

FOREWORD TO THE FIRST EDITION

These verses are a small tribute to the post-war decade, to the days when old cars were revered and new ones reviled, when you could see Fangio at Goodwood and could compete in your local hill-climb wearing a cloth cap.

It was a time of some confusion but of infinite enthusiasm. The clubs were just getting into their stride and none of them was as yet too large; the strong Bentley content of this book is a measure of the enormous amount of fun and good fellowship I myself found in the Bentley Drivers' Club.

Those years may lack the sheer romance of the Vintage Age but at least, after six years of war, we appreciated everything we got, whereas in the 'Twenties we took it all for granted. In these days of automation, nationalisation, and italianate pseudo-styling, we are unlikely ever to see such a time again.

Harry Charnock

CONTENTS

MERCEDES IN THE MIST

*This was the first motorcar verse I ever wrote, right back in
the Vintage Days.*

Out of the morning mist they came, hooded and goggled,
And the long proud bonnet before them, slender and
    silver;
Dew was on the shaggy fur of their coats and the folded
    windscreen
As silent they came and were gone with a swish of tyres.
And as they passed, I wondered to what place they
    journeyed,
No slut of a seaside town could it be; not the South of
    France,
Nor even the Pyrenees nor the Tyrol seemed meet to
    receive them.
Then I thought: They are voyagers from a remote planet,
Who have circled our world with the sun, stealing time
    from the day,
And now, speedier than light, travel outwards on
    causeways uncharted,
Bound for their parent star in the far void anchored.
And I pictured them climbing by winding ways of red
    sandstone,
Up to a stronghold supernal in its dark mountains,
With an alien moon swimming up into a sky of silver,
And in the castle walls red lights would spring out in
    welcome.
Up to the frowning gates would they come, to the
    drawbridge sinking
Slowly to span wet cliffs falling sheer into silence,
And over the bridge would they go and the great gates
    swallow
That peerless creature of silver, and the great bolts clang
    home.

THE SPORTSMAN AND THE BUSINESSMAN

The Sportsman and the Businessman were driving hub to
    hub,
The Sportsman to his office and the other to his club;
They cried 'The way these streets are packed amounts to a
    disgrace
'And so we blind that we may find a vacant parking
    place.'
They wriggled out of Market Cross and down the High
    Street broad,
A park attendant yawned 'We're full' in accents slightly
    bored.
A leader writer wrote a par on 'Roads we have outgrown,'
An idle cop hoped they would stop in some forbidden
    zone.

The light of battle in their eyes, they rattled up the town
And in and out the roundabout and out again and down,
Till in the middle distance, like a bright entrancing star,
A tiny space, a parking place for just a single car.

Feet down and into second gear they thundered up the
    street,
A fluster of jay walkers fled on swift and fearful feet,
A nonagarian lady with a shrewd and cunning face
just neatly eased her tricycle into that parking space.

       *   *   *

The Sportsman and the Businessman now leave their cars
    at home,
They park their motor scooters anywhere they go or come,
They both are glad to quit for good this damn fool parking
    game,
And how much better off we'd be if others did the same.

THE ALUMINIUM HEAD

Dedicated to those lovely ads which promise all the kingdoms
of the earth if you drink so-and-so at bedtime.

I bought an aluminium head,
It cost me several quid;
I don't know if the things they said
It did, it really did.

It nestled 'neath the bonnet,
Amid dead flies and grime,
And the silver sheen upon it
Was supernal and sublime.

It said 'You mean old' geezer
'Do you grudge me half-a-crown?
'Get busy with degreaser
'And clean this engine down.'

No job too filthy then to shirk,
I washed beneath the wings,
I made my trafficators work,
And even sprayed the springs.

Like reunited lovers,
My car and I were gay,
With radio, loose covers,
And a fifty quid respray.

The neighbours ceased to snicker,
At my lazy way of life;
Mrs. Doctor, Mrs. Vicar
Both called upon my wife.

At the office, the directors said,
'He's our best man by far;
'The other chaps drive round half dead
'Look how he keeps his car.'

And now I sit upon the Board,
And now lie late in bed;
How can I with mere words reward
My aluminium head?

ALL TOGETHER NOW

Oh carve this brief quotation
Above me when I'm dead:
'If you would gain salvation
'Get an aluminium head.'

OLD AUSTIN TEN

Welcome, scruffy little stranger to the Motor House
                                        Patrician,
Don't forget to wipe your sump upon the mat;
We who wear the faded laurels of the Paris Exposition
Cannot soil with tedious transport our superlative condition
When roads are crammed with common cars and weather
                                        is perdition;
They have brought you in to deal with things like that.

We are Vintage and Edwardian and polished to the eyes,
We are Restoration Drama, we are News,
And all the things you never were in quality and size,
Our pedigree is puncture-proof, our lines unshot with lies
And once a year we stagger forth to win a Concours prize;
But you they've got to use and use and use.

They've wrapped us up in cotton wool for close on
                                    twenty years,
What time you've passed through twenty pairs of hands;
While they kept us running sweetly with their toil and
                                    sweat and tears,
Exhorting us to emulate the fleet of Mr Seers,
You passed two hundred thousand and got no resounding
                                    cheers
But the same neglect an Austin understands.

We often talk among ourselves and wonder just for fun
If they'd bought a car like you back in the past
And changed the oil and ground the valves and used the
                                    greasing gun
Done all the things just as the, book says that they should
                                    be done
And never left you in the rain nor stood you in the sun,
How much longer than the rest of us you'd last.

Welcome scruffy little stranger to the menial tasks you
                                    know,
To the dirty trips demanded by our men,
To taking out and bringing back, dependable and slow;
Time comes when every one of us forsakes the status quo
To journey down that Dreadful Lane where dying motors
                                    go,
And wishes he'd been born an Austin Ten.

NEW YEAR'S EVE

This is not a motoring verse, but if you look closely you will find an Austin Seven.

The patent shoes are glossy bright,
The white carnation has its pin,
And double-ender snowy white
Beneath that pink and youthful chin;
The Vintage Seven waits within
Its aureole of lamplit rain,
Soon to announce with jovial din
He has a date with Julia Jane.

The blustering dark an arch of light,
All humankind beloved kin,
The worn old wheel is poised for flight,
And none can lose and all must win;
New worlds are waiting to begin
Around that turning of the lane,
Where, out beyond the planets' spin,
He has a date with Julia Jane.

Those mothers who are always right,
And fathers who are seldom in,
The maudlin playboy, loose or tight,
The treacly tart suffused with gin,
And all who sin or do not sin
Once more are young nor dare profane
That rapturous ecstatic grin;
He has a date with Julia Jane.

ENVOI
The tail lamps twinkle out of sight,
And memory surges back again,
Of thirty years ago tonight,
And of another Julia Jane.

SONNET FOR A FATHER

Do you remember how he scared you stiff
In that old car—but that was long ago;
Later he flew for years on ops and if
At last he went, it's how he'd wish to go.
You sold his clothes, his room became the spare,
But the green Bentley you would never sell,
Had it resprayed and plated, kept it there
Standing on blocks, the friend he'd known so well.

On summer evenings, when you cut the grass,
And Mother trims the borders with her shears,
The garage doors stand open, while there pass
Down your small garden all those golden years,
For two old people and a long green car
And one who hitched his Bentley to a star.

VALHALLA ROAD

Let them keep their four-stage rockets for what they may
        be worth,
And future aisles of atom-piles free-orbiting the earth,
That chain of cold space stations on the highway to a star,
When it is time to make my climb, I'd rather go by car.

When black and white comes out at last for man and weary
        wheel,
They'll dump this bod beneath the sod, but somehow then
        I feel
Old Behemoth, who shares the joys and burden of the
        past,
Perchance may wait beside that Gate where all men come
        at last.

His battery flat and cracked at that, and down at heel his
        springs,
But still upon his battered brow those proud untarnished
        wings,
Undaunted by corrosive time, untouched of rain and sun,
And game to face uncharted space as though it were A
        one.

By traffic streams once known in dreams we'll leave the
        moon behind,
Span the lumescent cliffs of stars in one all-glorious blind,
And just to see the Nebulae go round the longer way,
What's fifty million light-years more or less on such a day?

Till on our flight towards the night this galaxy shall glow,
Like London seen from Surrey hills where fog makes void
        below,
And no more cars and no more stars down the dark
        causeway come,
And icy loneliness blots out the glimmer that was home.

Then cosmic dust shall rack and rust an engine past its
      best,
No works, no spares department there, no parking place,
      no rest,
Flats without end and tubes to mend that ever leak apace,
And purgatory we may serve in that unholy place,

Until we reach those perfect roads where premium
      petrol's free,
With no patrols to pester souls to join the R.A.C.,
Where power curves don't flatten out and bikes in file
      behave,
And hug the grass and as you pass pedestrians cheer and
      wave.

And the Great Scrutineer Himself may turn to hide a smile,
As Behemoth swings on groaning springs down that last
      shining mile,
His engine full of piston slap, his driver packed with sin,
Yet may we dare seek welcome there and may they let us
      in

SONG OF THE OLD SMOKERS

We are rusty, musty, dusty but we still are hale and lusty,
Though we haven't got a virtue and we haven't got a clue;
We're the mimsers, we're the jokers, we're the horrible,
      Old Smokers
And they want to do away with us to leave the roads for
      you.

Our steering's not been castored since we hit that silly
      motorist
Upon A Three in Thirty Five, it really wasn't nice,

But we still get through the curly bits and wiggle up the
     whirly bits
Without an anti-roll bar or an anti-tramp device.

Our brakes may take a little time to bite through all the
     grease and grime,
We've no hydraulic lines to bust and put us on the spot,
But our roadholding in the wet is something that you can
     forget,
Unlike the current version of You Very Well Know What.

Though Ministers may well decide there's danger in our
     shaky ride,
There's nothing really wrong with us except that we are
     slow;
Executives must have their fling along the Preston Motor
     thing
At twenty-five above the ton-and so we've got to go.

When your alligator bonnet won't retain the catch upon it,
When your wrap-round windshield shatters or you get a
     tubeless burst,
When pseudoplastic leatherette through pressed steel roof
     is soaking wet,
When your Trumpery takes a corner and the corner gets
     there first.

All broken into shapeless lumps or piled in rusting rubbish
     dumps,
Reclaimed from scrap as good as new or stacked on
     breakers' shelves,
The ghosts of the Old Smokers, those irreverent old jokers,
Will be laughing, laughing, laughing fit to bust among
     themselves.

NIGHT RIDE—3 a.m.

Before the waking hour, too late for slumber,
Between the midnight and the unborn day,
In twilit green twin Jaeger fingers number,
Lumescent figures meaningless as they;
The lonely engine note is lilting thunder,
The landmarks loose their lines and melt away
As ancient dreams lace weariness with wonder,
And thought spans farther far than wise men say.
By flamethrown beams on curling catseyes gleaming,
The plunging tarmac tunnels out of night,
Winds on beyond the utmost verge of seeming
To where, on wheels of energy and light,
Down lanes of stars the small dark worlds are streaming,
To cosmic cities infinite and bright.

IN MEMORIAM, JEAN PIERRE MARECHAL
LE MANS, 1949

Now we will think of you, the sun is setting
To sweep another land with ambient light,
The charming things you did are past forgetting,
Your few small wrongs shall vanish with the night.

The chequered flag is furled, the while we wonder
On what far circuit even now you fare
To mock the sullen stars with lilting thunder,
The winds of space to whip your flying hair.

The airfields and the roads of England knew you
Who drove for England your few fleeting years;
We who remember raise our glasses to you,
For you deserve more honour than our tears.

YOUNG ENGLAND

Cor wotasmasher Mister; coo, Mister, wottleshedo?
I've brort me little sister and me cousin Sebastian too,
Fer Mum's gorn orf to the pitchers, and Dad 'e's doin' 'is
　　pools,
So we've come aht to play wiv yer motor 'cos it's 'oliday
　　time at the schools.

And when you and yer bird's gorn orf soppy, and you've
　　left yer car in the park,
Then me and me bruvvers and several uvvers won't 'arf
　　'ave noendofalark;
I'll be the Space Ship Capting and me sister the Maiden
　　from Mars
Wot rides supersomics just like in the comics, only we 'as
　　ter do it wiv cars.

Young Ernie can write orl the rude words 'e knows on the
　　screen where it's covered wiv dust,
And as Annie can't read she can play wiv the wiper
　　(she 'as, and the flippin' thing's bust)
While Baby's quite 'appy just sitting up 'ere wiv 'undreds
　　of switches ter pull,
And Perce strikes a match by the 'ole in yer tank ter see
　　if the perisher's full.

But there's a bloke 'aving a puncture, so it's time ter be
　　going fer us
To give 'im advice till 'e's dotty, but ta fer the use of
　　yer bus,
And if Mum gives me 'arf of a bloater wot's stayed in the
　　larder too long,
I'll tie it on top of yer motor, it won't 'arf make
　　noendofapong.

SMALL AD.

Impoverished motor has to sell
One owner-driver, grand old lot,
Smokes far too much, but goes like hell,
Blood pressure, seven hundred, hot.

Frame slightly bent in wartime crash,
Rheumatic shackle, offside rear,
Turbulent head gives bags of dash
On any premium grade of beer.

Bearing (with women) slightly loose,
But clean from recent overhaul,
Free will (of very little use)
And overdraft (no use at all).

Ugly old body, strongly built,
All minor rattles can be cured,
Taxed for the year (up to the hilt)
And comprehensively inured.

Motor regrets he must be rid
Of this superb old vintage soak,
Best offer over twenty quid,
Swap, cash adjustment, cheaper bloke.

THE THREE VINTAGES OF P.A.

1949—rough and fruity.
They're belting out of Hangar Straight,
They're sliding into Stowe,
And some are daft and some are scared
And all are bloody slow.
Now A has lost his virtue
And B has lost a pot,
And C has clouted everything
With everything he's got,
While D is tangled in his beard
And even E has slowed
(Small wonder, while he's driving
That obstreperous 'commode),
And so they vanish out of sight,
Save those who've lost their way,
The biggest bunch of gormless clots
That I have seen today.

1951—extra sweet.
Magnificently bungled, sir,
Superlatively spun,
How true you smote those silly drums,
Encore, bravo, well done.
What faultless virtuosity
On dire and deadly Stowe,
All splendid chaps on splendid cars,
Oh jolly splendid show!

1953—triple sec.
Good afternoon, ladies and gentlemen, the races have
begun.
Good evening, ladies and gentlemen, the races have been
run.

SHOWROOM, W.1.

We are the ultimate sophistication
Where displaced politicians pawn their Rolls,
Devoted members of the Hogwasch combine,
Bless their aesthetic altruistic souls.

Our salesmen are aloof and unapproachable
For selling cars is scarcely their concern,
Our typists have such devastating uplift
When they stand up they nearly overturn.

Our clientele, exalted as our carriages,
Yet more distinction to our calling gives,
Those bleak-faced bods who fiddle foreign currency,
Nationalised tycoons and super-spivs.

Our chaste and plate-glass precincts brook no mention
Of such vulgarities as motor clubs;
Our atmosphere, pile carpets, condescension,
Dry sherry, leather chairs and palms in tubs.

A motorcar is merely incidental
In this rare haunt of elegance and ease;
We recognise the Wraith, the Continental,
But never even speak of Phantom Threes.

Mark Sixes slightly used from seven thousand
Of course come cheaper if you buy them new,
But then the Hogwasch Group is so exclusive,
To deal becomes a privilege for you.

Big Bores enhance each urbane situation
Where Firm's Expenses seem an act of faith
To brighten up a semi-bankrupt nation
Whose better days are still a silver wraith.

Devoted members of the Hogwasch combine,
We can ignore the rude plebeian wit
Of Gorgeous Cars; we also may be twisters,
But we at least can get away with it.

CORNISH SONG

London Apprentice, Nancenoy, Indian Queen and Par,
The names are enough to give you joy or ever you take
    your car,
Perranzabuloe, Come to Good, Luxulian, Looe,
    Gunwalloe;
        I bust a propshaft on Bodmin Moor,
        It cried 'Oh find me an open door'
        And it made a damned great hole in the floor
        For Hardy and Spicer to follow.

You can fiddle more than the Helston Flora any day of the
    week
In Perranarworthal, Constantine, Probus, Polperro,
    Gweek,
And sow wild oats in a flower-lit lane at the age of
    ninety-three,
        For the hills go up and the hills go down
        And the streets are so narrow in Mousehole
            town
        When you squeeze in the gutter you drive on
            the crown,
        And reversing means putting to sea.

At holiday times there are clots galore on the roads as well
      as the cream,
Down to Land's End and back they go in a
      follow-my-leader dream,
But peace still sleeps along Frenchman's Creek, in St.
      Tudy, Porthloe and Paul;
           When I hit that Bump outside St. Blazey
           I.F.S. would have gone plumb crazy,
           But the old cart spring said 'Oopsidaisy'
           And shed a few leaves, that's all.

London Apprentice, Nancenoy, Indian Queen and Par,
Lostwithiel sinks in the mists astern, in the wake of an
      early star;
Seven counties have shed their dust on our British Racing
      Green,
           And Tony is cooking a fabulous chop,
           We will sit in the bar and talk motoring shop,
           The fug will thicken and Time shall stop
           Till to-morrow shall never have been.

BORE WISE, PISTON FOOLISH

Little Willie's racing pistons
Were the joy of his existence
But the rings within their grooves
Made too many wasteful moves,
Letting noxious gases pump
Down into the seething sump,
Sloshing stygian oil in quarts
In and out the carboned ports;
Though there could be no dissent
That little Willie's motor went,
Still, like many mugs before,
He splashed the cash on a rebore.

Little Willie's jampot pistons
Are the bane of his existence;
Oil consumption now is nil,
So is power on a hill,
Bores and rings each other squeezing,
Overheating, melting, seizing,
Paving Willie's road to hell
With graphite and with U.C.L.;
His engine will be nice and free
Some time in 1963.

What a lot of things to spoil
To save a little drop of oil.

IDYLL IN SUBURBIA

Some men contrive to go like Eno's
On tiny scalded Topolinos
To Berlin, Paris, Rome, Madrid
Without once lifting up the lid,
Or to outstrip the blue beyond
Steered by a few c.c. of Bond,
But I need ninety B.H.P.
To battle through to E.C.3
From Cobham, Cheshunt, where you will,
From Penge or Harrow-on-the-Hill.
I cannot use this power at all
Where under-scheduled buses crawl,
The cost of it is past disputing,
The time I save not worth computing,
While seats with room for three or four
Contain my brief-case, nothing more.
Why do it when, you rightly ask,
A minicar performs the task?

Why are new models made galore
Unless to rile the folks next door,
Or General Motors plan their Sabre
Save to impress some envious neighbour?
Each morning close on half-past eight,
Black Homburg on my worthy pate,
Each eve upon low-pressure feet
I give the watching road a treat,
My coachwork shines, my ego swells
And muted conscience never tells
That, minus my enchromiumed steed,
I am a little man indeed.

POET UP PRESCOTT

After a mixed evening of Robert Browning and
"Motor Sport"

We are down in the Paddock all golloping tea,
I gollop, he gollops, she gollops with me;
Then I warm up my motor, what power I've had it give
With anti-detergent inhibited additive,
Add a jubilee clip to the crack in the steering arm,
(Let him sneer all he will for how can his sneering harm?)
Detect of my sparking plugs which isn't and which is,
(How can I have trodden on Stubberfield's sandwiches?)
Then I sweep to the line and I come to a stop,
Clutch out, handbrake on, and gear lever in top.
"In top?" say you truly; it has been much worse,
For once I took off with the thing in reverse.
Rise of revs, fall of flag, and in with the clutch,
It stutters, it stalls, there is death in my touch.
Oh find me a gear in the gearbox, I pray,
Third, second, to first and AWAY.

Then up, ever upward I snarl to the blue,
There goes half a valve and a collet or two,
I am under the bridge, I am down in the drain,
I am back on the road, I am off it again;
That is not Castrol R you can smell, it is—Pardon,
I am eating an onion I picked in the garden.
But is she at the Esses, all watchful for me,
Or down in the Paddock still golloping tea
With him, bugattistical atrophied ape,
May his cam-contours wither his crank out of shape?

Now number four piston has gone through the bonnet,
Mark well how the sunlight is shining upon it,
My tyres are in tatters, the friction is meltin' 'em,

I am into the Esses, I'm half way to Cheltenham,
My vizor's in flames, I have swallowed a starling,
But *there* on the bank is my angel, my darling.

Tears gush from my eyes like the spirit from bowsers,
The layshaft has lodged in the seat of my trousers;
Where an old tonneau cover has patched them is fair torn,
But what care I for that who, inflated and airborne,
No longer am victim of doubts and distresses
For she clomb through the mud to watch me through the
    Esses?

Pulses, once wild, have with all life to burn slowed;
And my car, by itself, goes back down the return road.

WHITSUN ROUT

Whitsuntide is on the way,
Come and join the Whitsun rout,
Traffic sense put by to-day,
Trafficators hanging out.

Down the highway to the sea
All of wheel-borne England rushes;
Junior, it seems to me,
Needs a visit to the bushes.

By this blind and hump-backed curve,
Stands a most convenient gate,
Brake so hard we slide and swerve,
Junior can seldom wait.

Cycling club behind has bid
For a motorist's reproof,
Two are on the luggage grid,
Three have landed on the roof.

Motor cyclist (who's annoyed him?)
Hits our open door's front edge,
Mighty Daimler to avoid him
Founders gently in the hedge.

Scarlet motor coach that follows
Earns a glorious smack behind
And an Austin Seven swallows;
You would think they all were blind.

For a mile the bumpers touch,
Everybody hoots and pushes,
Auntie May has laughed so much
She must also seek the bushes.

Drivers good there are not many,
They don't know what they're about;
junior has spent his penny,
We rejoin the Whitsun rout.

INCIDENT

The valley brims with twilight, gold lamps prick out the
    town,
The shadows creep like grazing sheep across the darkening
    Down,
The headlight ribbon flickers from the homing throng of
    cars,
And the road you took from London was your highway to
    the stars.

Your T.T. Replica squashed flat on that retaining wall,
And chaps have rushed to fetch the police and ambulance
    and all,
The cyclist who had no rear lamp is drinking at the
    Crown,
And the callous clot who did not dip is halfway back to
    Town.

UNSOLICITED TESTIMONIAL

My dear old boy, I'm not a motor snob,
But since I've had my car I must confess
The Schnitzel Group have done a lovely job
With their Q Thirty-Seven hyphen S.

Suspension feather soft and so refined
Front tyres will last three thousand, often more,
And twice as far ere brakes must be relined,
And thrice before one thinks of a rebore.

Their service is superb as well I know,
Who am familiar with their service shop
Where reconditioned engines come and go
Because they will not go or will not stop.

Starters burn out and, presto, there arrive
New starters to burn out another day
And after six months' use the final drive
Is full of youthful and exuberant play.

My dear old boy, think what it used to be,
The Twenties, when some firms so low would stoop
To give their cars a five-year guarantee,
But then, alas, we had no Schnitzel Group.

CLUB WIVES

They gather in the farther bar,
A closely cordoned ring,
And watch their husbands air their views
On anything that's in the news
Pertaining to, the sporting car
Or any motor thing.

Let someone bring a girl along
Who talks the language too,
Who chatters to the nearest chap
Of understeer and overlap,
The claws are sharp, the claws are strong
For work they have to do.

But should some sportsman like a lamb,
With understanding eye
Discourse to these same wives of all
The things which women most enthral,
The husbands never give a damn——
I often wonder why.

SONG OF THE WIPER

Flip Flop, Flip Flop,
Never falter, never stop,
Through mist and mud and sleet and snow
On and on and on I go,
The same by night and the same by day,
Chucking the raindrops out of the way;
Call it an easy job but, Lord,
A chap gets stiff and a chap gets bored
With the same old swish and the same old slop,
Flip Flop, Flip Flop.

Flip Flop, Flip Flop,
Waiting for the rain to stop;
Everything else has some sort of a range,
The gearbox gets no end of a change,
Carburettors choke and cough,
The lights go on and the lights go off,
Tyres can go to soft from hard,
Even the spark can advance and retard,
But I go on until I drop,
Flip Flop, Flip Flop.

If I might indulge in a skip, and a hop
Such as Flip Flop, Flipperty Flop,
Or even the tiniest ghost of a skip
Like Flop Flop, or Flip Flip,
That at least would something be
To break this damned monotony,
But never a chance, I keep on turning,
Gears gone dry and windings burning,
Till my armature goes pop,
Flip Flop, Flip Flop.

JOSEPHINE

Josephine was too terrific,
Aphrodisiac, calorific,
When she sidled through the bar
No man talked about his car,
And scruffy types forsook their ales
To scrub their scruffy finger nails,
While none delayed to pay his sub
When she joined our motor club.

The trousered corrugated bints
Who did their stuff in climbs and sprints,
And prissy numbers versed in trials,
With mud upon their homely dials,
Said 'Just you wait, the Ladies' Cup
'Will show this flouncing floozie up,
'And scrambles circuit bring declension
'To her pneumatic front suspension.'

The Ladies' Cup, as oft before,
Took place in rain and sleet galore,
And anxious marshals watched their wives
Risk precious cars in power dives
On terrain where the mud and snow
Proved far too much for little Jo,
Who foundered in a freezing brook;
But still that girl had what it took.

For not a man upon the brink
But headlong plunged into the drink,
Leaving that section unobserved
And all the other girls unnerved,

Some of whom sank without a trace
Or backward quit the loathly place,
But all agreed that Josephine
Had pulled a stratagem unclean.

Meanwhile the men, their hearts aglow,
Bore homeward dripping happy Jo
Who learnt, and not at all distressed,
She'd lost more marks than all the rest;
But chaps, who thought this such a pity,
Co-opted her to the Committee,
And now committee meetings run
Six hours instead of barely one.

The moral is you shouldn't squeal
If other girls have sex-appeal,
And you may lose a man's affections
If he observes your non-stop sections.

HILL CLIMB 1921

A genial policeman saunters in the sun;
From the green Paddock, under hawthorns, pass
Akela, Brescia, Horstmann, one by one,
With pungent castor haze and burnished brass.
The Maytime afternoon is molten glass
And he who blips unwisely is undone,
Our makeshift timing tangles in the grass
And Raymond Mays is on his practice run.

Gold midges dust across the slanting sun,
Down the cool Paddock hawthorn shadows crawl,
The hard exhausts diminish, rasp and fall,
A grey road beckons for the homeward run;
Fold up, for precious memories, your fun
And grab your gown and clatter into Hall.

THE GREAT CAR DUMP, ADVERSANE

The field drops gently northward; from the road
You do not see what rests the other side
The grassy hulks, with bonnets gaping wide,
The stricken Ghost beneath its bramble load.
Lambda, Lorraine and Lanchester, denied
Forever now the highways once bestrode,
Reap not the mileage their designers sowed
But huddle here in timeless eventide.

Creep through the hedge, beneath this broken wire,
Bring all the tools to shift that rusted head,
And when you have the spares you so desire,
Sit here and commune with the mighty dead,
And think, as daylight sinks from rose to grey,
How something of those hearts beats on to-day.

COMBUSTIO AD INFERNUM

I knew a man who loved Mercedes
More than liquor, lucre, ladies,
Wore the proud three-pointed star
On tie as well as motorcar,
On handkerchief and undervest
And, in tattoo, upon his chest.

One day he chanced an inn to pass
And, pausing there to sink a glass,
Found in this unpretentious pub
Headquarters of the Occult Club.
Behind that door marked Ales and Beers
Sat sorcerers and subtle seers,
Merlins, unnaturally aspirated,
With phantoms who associated,
And wizard types who played the host,
To any interesting ghost.

The three-point star, the SSK,
These worthies saw and straight away,
Knowing but little of Mercedes,
They judged he came direct from Hades,
And quit their necromantic tryst
Exclaiming 'Look, a Poltergeist.'
They pressed upon him brandies, gins,
Exhorted him to tell his sins,
If he had ever been in ditches,
And what about the local witches,
And if that night he would unsheath
Demonic doings on the heath.

That he be judged a bod satanic
Caused in our friend a major panic;
These men might turn his Merc-mit-blower
Into a twelve-inch Atco mower,
Or else abandon him to fate
In Dagenharn's dire Consulate,
So, when they called to him at eve
'Oh murky brother, we believe
'Our alchemy is poor enough,
'Pull out the stops and do your stuff.
'We modest men perchance would barter
'Our starting up without the starter
'For magic of such violent types
'As lurks within your organ pipes,'
He answered 'Chums, I must, I fear,
'Get to the hell right out of here,'
Which happy phrase they all acclaimed,
Agreeing he could not be blamed.

The starter clanged, the blower blew,
The m.p.g. went up the flue,
He vanished as a demon must
In smoke and flames and rubber dust.

But when there came the morning light,
Black cellulose had turned to white;
just how, he finds it hard to name,
His car's been never quite the same,
But still the three-point star he toasts,
Avers his disbelief in ghosts,
And blames as cause of all he's seen,
Too much Mercedes Benzedrine.

A ZERO

A One goes up to Doncaster,
A Four to Avonmouth,
A Three goes down to Pompey Town;
East, North and West and South

The web spins out from London
By smooth arterial ways,
But through them all A Zero weaves
The thread of other days.

It dodges all the traffic lights,
No roundabouts it meets;
It goes by little leafy squares
And little secret streets,

It winds from cobbled London,
Where the horse-drawn traffic jams,
To the clopping of the hansom
And the rattle of the trams,

Where fog is never far away
And throaty bulb-horns blow,
Out to waterbound macadam
For the wheels of long ago.

Along its dusty surface
The Humber dog-cart bowls,
The Motosacoche, the Bradbury,
The Berliet, the Rolls.

A chiffon motor-veil goes by
Beneath the chestnut buds
To music of great singing chains
And tyres with metal studs,

And will she boil on Kingston Hill,
And will she reach the top,
And will she ever start again
If once we let her stop?

The Bobby is our enemy,
The blacksmith is our friend,
But every journey perilous
Clanks somehow to its end.

And in a knickerbocker suit,
Perched high on dickey seat,
A schoolboy sees the genesis
Of strange and flying feet.

*   *   *

Four hours to get to Doncaster
And two to Pompey Town
On black and perfect bitumen
Where nothing lets you down.

If you will but behave yourself
The traffic cop's your friend,
And every journey commonplace
Has little save its end.

But sometimes in the evening
When daily trips are done,
A Zero beckons from a past
Beyond the bygone sun.

And he who, as a schoolboy,
Perched high on dickey seat,
Would give ten thousand miles and more
For one brief sortie sweet

On waterbound macadam,
On tyres with metal studs,
Where magic and adventure went
Beneath the chestnut buds.

MONOGRAMANIA

The badge on the bar on the front of your car
Is to-day just a thought mediocre,
And if you have a passion to be in the fashion,
You must wear it on blazer or choker.

For a girl it looks better on headscarf or sweater
And, if she is up to the minute,
The design on her bra tells the name of the car
Beloved of the bosom within it.

One-make panoramas on nylon pyjamas
Will soon be a masculine trimming,
Or in waterproof plastic tied on with elastic,
Worn over the navel while swimming.

That you don't need a car for your badges and bar
Should make you both richer and gladder,
And if some foreign cad says the English are mad,
By Gad, sir, they're now a bit madder.

CAVEAT VENDITOR

That little ad. was quite a gem,
By Friday there'll be queues of them
Right down the road all keen to buy
But Friday comes and passes by.

On Tuesday week the blower blows,
A chap who knows a chap who knows
A chap who wants a car like mine
Will come on Sunday sharp at nine.
Comes Sunday morning, bottled ale
Stands by to seal a happy sale;
Comes ten, eleven, twelve and one,
Our car stands wilting in the sun,
And then, at three, they all arrive;
A dreadful vehicle blocks our drive
Cascading children, Mum and Dad,
('A job to find this place we've had'),
Two shaggy dogs our peace invade,
And Uncle, who is in the Trade.

The children plant unerring feet
On precious blooms and borders neat,
Those dreadful dogs assail our cat,
Says Dad 'A fine old bus is that,'
Says Mum 'A lovely place you've got,'
Says Uncle 'Where's the you-know-what?'
A harrassed wife dispenses tea
And then forgets a cup for me,
And in this bedlam I must try
To get the silly clot to buy.

I press the knob, the starter whirrs,
The starter jams, and Uncle purrs,
I croak 'She's not done this before,'
Untie the bendix; with a roar
My lovely engine comes to life,
Brings brats and dogs and portly wife
Of trial run to claim their shares.
Somehow the tonneau-cover tears,
The handbrake locks where Uncle clutched it,
(It was all right until he touched it),
Dad tries the wiper, leaves a wreck,
Those dogs are breathing down my neck;
And, as for the main road we slow,
Uncle decides he'll have go.

He splays his rump and hulking feet
In my familiar driving seat
Which for his bulk does not adjust,
And when it does, the slide is bust;
Bangs in the clutch, the motor stalls,
With merriment the family-bawls.
Away at last, from one to two
He gaily chips a cog or two,
He misses third, we nearly stop,
Then slams the lever into top,
Says 'These old jobs are tricky runners,
'I'm more at home with twenty-tonners.'

Back home, says Mum 'It's time to go,'
Calls Uncle 'We will let you know'
And, as he clips my garden gate,
'We really want a Morris Eight.'

SCRIPTOR OMNIPOTENS

I visited the Works to view
The promised Mark Eighteen;
They said 'Old boy, it's good of you,
'Have lunch in our canteen.'
They praised my journalistic tripe,
They lushed me up with ale,
I drove home in the prototype
And wrote a lovely tale
In which I praised the Mark Eighteens
With rich purpureal par—
And several thousand Argentines
Have bought a lousy car.

Then I went down another day
To view the new Mark Twenty;
They said 'For Pete's sake run away,
'Upon our plate we've plenty,
'Le Mans, the Alpine and the Show,
'About enough for us.
'Be a good fellow, up and go.'
So I went home by bus
And wrote some vitriolic lines
Their confidence to jar—
And several thousand Argentines
Have missed a lovely car.

LAMENT

I do not like the motorcar at all,
It has destroyed the tempo of my life,
Its oil has spoiled the Wilton in the hall
And livened up the temper of my wife.

Without it, at canasta or at bridge
Might I have won prestige or even prizes,
Or fishing, known caress of cramp and midge,
Hit, thrown or booted balls of various sizes.

Shot at small birds that never did me harm,
Rid garden plot of buttercup and groundsel,
Or kept my bottom dignified and warm
Seated upon the Rural District Council.

Such worthy tasks, and there are many others,
Might I have served and, glorious consummation,
Found company amid those jovial brothers
Of the Pedestrians' Association.

Instead I chose the stony garage path,
Bartered clean finger nails and flannel bags
For B.H.P., whose only aftermath
Is rear end views of Nashes and of Jags.

The tank is empty and the battery dead,
Bills shower on the Wilton in the hall,
An overdraft blows chill about my head,
I do not like the motorcar at all.

ELEGY FOR CLEANING RAGS

I keep a rag-bag on the garage wall,
Replete with miscellaneous odds and ends,
Which, when spring-cleaning looms upon us all,
Swells up with things so worn that no one mends.

That sporting shirt of soft Glenurquhart checks,
Bought hopelessly in Autumn '39,
And junior's prepschool pants, now tangled wrecks,
But good for making aluminium shine.

Pyjamas, once deserving of encomium,
To burnish sump, immaculate from Gunk,
Old nylons, unsurpassed for glass and chromium,
Once-precious fabrics, now discarded junk.

And when the springtime, opening her door,
Bestirs the ageing Bentley in its sleep,
I tumble out upon the garage floor
The bygone years in one chromatic heap.

A blazer, with the badge torn out from it,
A khaki handkerchief with ink defaced,
These that I loved and wore until they split,
And that which surely once her trousseau graced.

Call me romantic moron if you will
Who to disturb the sleeping past abhors;
Once more the rag-bag to its limit fill
And go and buy some dusters at the Stores.

RHAPSODY IN REAR WINDOWS

When driving in dense traffic queues
How often do we find
Preceding cars' rear-window views
Do not instruct nor yet amuse
But hypnotise and mesmerise,
Sometimes damn nearly paralyse
With rage the chap behind.

A transfer may be there which says
The Courteous Drivers' Club
Has here a member who obeys
The Highway Code's didactic phrase,
The very whiteness of whose rightness
Answers our commonplace politeness
With a scathing snub.

A pendant plastic dicky-bird,
A woolly pussy-cat,
The dog that howls, thank God, unheard,
Or Auntie's hat, obscene, absurd,
The features red, unkempt, unfed,
Of darling little tousle-head
(Or snotty little brat).

And if, by urgent law, the rear
Window be rendered free
Of all these horrors which appear,
Giving their driver vision clear
Of those who try past him to pry,
Would he pull in and let them by?
Not on your life, not he.

BAT OUT OF HELL

The big hand wavers close on five,
The oil on sixty plus,
The front end seems to come alive
To have its fun with us.

The summer air is solid lumps,
The road, once broad and fair,
A convex funnel sprouting bumps
Which are not really there.

Just as we think we're rather clever
And must tell our friends,
The straight we thought went on for ever
Sickeningly ends.

The smooth right-hander tightens fast,
Out anchors, shorten sail——
Do men condemned review their past?—
Round comes the ruddy tail.

Left rudder; far too much, you ass;
Now right hand down, you oaf;
We wouldn't now be on the grass
If you had used your loaf.

It's jolly still to be alive,
The tankard soon we'll lift
And tell how we, at ninety-five,
Achieved a faultless drift.

FOR ALL DRIVERS

Now bring her down off the crown to the leaf-strewn
    gutter,
Potter along where the slim blue shadows fall
And, lifting your foot, let the muttering tailpipe utter
Its blessings upon the lordliest sport of all.

On the odd little man in the cluttering family Seven,
On the pseudo-dicer in bogus racing green,
The vintagent braving outrageous rains of heaven,
On Yank and utility, midget and limousine.

One in the toil and the cost, in despair and glory,
Enemies often, but ultimate brothers at heart,
Speak each our piece in the long enchanting story,
Burn up our ration of road and then depart.

And those who, centuries hence, shall follow after,
When the day of the piston-engined car is done,
As they muse on our one-time nonsense may quell their
    laughter,
And murmur 'Fools, but by heaven they had their fun.'

HORSELESS SAVAGES

There are queues upon the by-roads and the wind is in
    the west,
This is carnival, fiesta, gala day and all the rest;
It will rain like hell by nightfall, there are no more parking
    spaces,
Bring out your fancy dress, my dears, we're going to the
    races.

Now he who goes to Ascot must sartorially behave,
But who follows motor racing shall have fashion for his
    slave;
Cobalt and orange dancing shirt in lieu of trim cravat,
And in Auntie's velvet pelmet are the makings of a hat.
What matter if we have no hood and only aero-screens,
As long, as last year's lilac slacks are this year's ginger
    jeans?
So, don that mad sombrero, those emerald corduroys,
And join the motor racing rout with all the girls and boys,
With popsys in sunbathing tops where little top remains,
And rosy cherubs in M.G.'s with pipes and growing pains,
Rough numbers clad in sailcloth shorts or dingy dungarees,
And smooth ones in petunia pants too tight to bend their
    knees,
Old rakes with leather faces and girls with prison crops
And little chaps with woolly manes and sprouting
    mutton-chops.

There goes the Ace of Knaves who takes the wrong side of
the road,
The Clot of Clubs whose badge-bar crumples underneath
its load,
Pomp and Circumstance Number One, the caustic
motor-writer,
And the B.R.M. Supporters making faces at the blighter,
Surrealist Sue whose ear-rings once held down an Alta
head,
And Mucky Dan who motors in the clothes he wears in
bed.

Thank God for all eccentrics and that places still remain
Where only racing drivers look comparatively sane;
We've pinking Pool and purchase tax and bureaucrats
and all,
We've our backs against the grindstone and our noses to
the wall,
The beer is never what it was and we've abandoned
smoking,
By now we need retreading and respraying and decoking,
But as long as there's a wheel of sorts to hold, it is enough
To queue the whole damn day to watch the dicers do
their stuff.

Who dares say England's decadent, and how can England
die
While her purple beards and headscarves stream in glory
down the sky,
And while her sons and daughters take, undaunted and
unblown,
The wrong way back from Goodwood on the road to
Silverstone?

TOAST FOR A SUPER SALESMAN

There's sawdust in the gearbox,
There is gear-oil in the sump,
A lump of grease as hard as cheese
Packs out the water-pump.

The rad. is full of Neverleak,
The crank is round the bend,
Insulting tape and rubber crepe
From wilting wires depend.

There's chewing gum around the tank,
Resprayed as good as new,
While on the heads' distorted threads
Are gobs of metal glue.

The perforated Brooklands Can
With laughter loud beguiles,
And oval bores have kept the scores
For ninety thousand miles.

But chromium polish does a lot,
And Brasso does the rest;
If love be blind and fate be kind
Some mug should be impressed.

So, up with elbows, hearties all,
And down the hatch it slips;
We toast with grace the whiskered face
That launched a thousand snips.

PROGRESS

The Nausea Six of '53
Is on the production line;
The proud Works Manager said to me
'She's as perfect a car as a car can be,
'We've learnt quite a lot since '33
'About up-to-date design.'

I've a Nausea Six of '33,
As good as any I've seen;
The m.p.h. and the m.p.g.,
The Standing Quarter and B.H.P.
Are almost the same as for '53,
So what have they done between?

Too much room for your bottom and none for your feet,
And suspension by flexible wires;
The curve in the windscreen is awfully neat,
It reflects in your eyes every lamp in the street
While you corner in comfort and slide on the seat
To the signature tune of the tyres.

The speedometer lives in a strange device,
The ammeter's gone for a Burton,
The interior heater warms up in a trice
So it gives you the chance of pneumonia twice,
But as long as the plastic finish is nice,
The success of the motor is certain.

The double-dip beam turns night into day,
Or that's how it seems to be
To the poor sap coming the opposite way,
And the seats fold into a bed they say,
So boys and girls come out to play
In the Nausea '53.

The Nausea Six of '54
Is in the designer's brain;
Will he offer us blobular tin galore,
Where virtue was ever its own rebore,
Or will he go back twelve years and more
To give us a car again?

WINTER SPORTSMEN

When circuits are deserted
And in pubs the drivers meet,
When Silverstone is swathed in fog
And Goodwood drowned in sleet,

As autumn turns to winter,
To brighten up our day,
The motor periodicals
A picture then display.

It may change a bit in detail
But it's always much the same;
It shows a slimy dank ravine
With some disgusting name,

The Sog, the Squelch, the Spattermuck,
Dead Hole or Poison Ghyll;
Pray curb your nausea, reader dear,
They mean it is a hill.

Up this ascent a vehicle crawls,
By Barrow out of Pram,
For friction, gravity and all
It does not give a damn.

The rear wheels wallow deep in ooze,
The front ones paw the air,
The thing's peculiar shape precludes
An engine anywhere.

Perchance those cylinders behind
Propel with Calor gas,
Or sets of pedals we might find
Deep down in the morass.

The portly pilot beams goodwill,
He seems to work a lot,
His passenger is fatter still
And bounces on his bot.

And when they reach the barren crest
Their task is not yet done,
But seek they ever, without rest,
An even steeper one,

Till such a slimy depth appears
Of quagmire unfrequented,
They vanish all but eyes and ears,
Then go home well contented.

But do not mock these gentlemen
Nor judge their pastime dim,
Unless you can yourself endure
Conditions half as grim.

TOUJOURS LA POLITESSE

'Excuse me, but your Trafficator's showing.'
'Forgive me, I forgot to tuck it in.'
'Your pardon, Madam, which way are you going?'
'My thanks, kind Sir, to turn I will begin.

'To left—no, right—or is it left, I wonder?'
'Pray take your time, dear lady, while I pass.'
'No—it is right. Oh, what a shocking blunder.
'Now your car is up a lamp-post on the grass!'

'Your forgiveness, Madam, if I did unnerve you,
'Let us blame the road, my driving or the fog.
'My shattered car and I are here to serve you,
'And here a lamp-post for your little dog.'

'Oh gallant Sir, I would have thought that never
'Could man with such rare chivalry behave;
'My car, my dog are yours—and I, for ever
'Your servant, Sir, and your adoring slave.'

. . . MAIS PAS TOUJOURS

All others of the road you are depriving,
May you wither, may you perish, may you rot!
I thought as much-it is a woman driving,
The cretinous incalculable clot.

A lesson to remember I will teach her,
I will pass her on this corner, going slow,
Shake both my fists in fury as I reach her
And bellow all the rudest words I know.

Now am I level with my wretched quarry-
A vehicle looms from nowhere-oh alas!
I've hit the woman's wing, I've hit a lorry,
And my car is up a lamp-post on the grass!

How can admonition end in such a manner,
How can dignity so suddenly decrease?
Here comes the lorry driver with a spanner,
Here comes the angry woman with the police.

THE SEVEN AGES OF SMALL ADS.

Stark and delightful Frazer Nash,
Highly tuned and sporting,
Exchange two-seater, doors and hood,
(Owner busy courting).

M.G. in mint condition,
Will never fail or falter,
Exchange for something with a roof,
(Owner at the altar).

Superlative short sports saloon,
Acceleration vivid,
Exchange cash, Carry-cot and pram,
(Owner pretty livid).

Pram, play-pen, baby-bath, layette,
And lots of other stuff,
Exchange for roomy vintage car,
(Owner had enough).

Collapsed and breathless old barouche,
Coachwork somewhat funny,
Exchange with cash Mark Eight or Nine,
(Owner in the money).

Magnificent drophead de luxe,
A car to rave about,
Exchange for something soft and slow,
(Owner wearing out).

Patrician pompous limousine,
Sedate and safe and sound,
Heir will exchange for Frazer Nash,
(Owner underground).

WOMAN'S ANGLE

He is with Her; the frowning garage portal
Forbids me now to threaten or implore;
Only remains, to show he still is mortal,
An oily-handled teacup on the floor.

The hirsute grass pleads mutely for the mower
And other wives laugh gaily with their men,
But they have not acquired a worn out blower
Nor sought to fit it to a Gormless Ten.

My piteous Sunday joint, uncooked, unheeded,
With Monday's laundering now must interfere;
Let shoes go dirty, flower beds unweeded,
As long as Vulcan gets his bottled beer.

We might have gone to Mother's, oiled the mangle,
Unstopped the sink or fixed the kitchen shelves
But men don't understand the woman's angle,
They only think of motors and themselves.

Each sunlit hour becomes to me a menace,
The man at Number Four repaints his gate,
While in her new M.G. takes off for tennis,
That tarty creature down at Number Eight,

While here in Number Six I wait and wonder
Why Sunday papers more than others pall,
Till, as the garage doors burst wide asunder,
He tramples oil marks all about the hall.

Leaves the wash basin with a greasy inset,
Demands his food and slaps me on the back,
(Damp dingy prints upon my precious twin set),
And on loose covers signs his seat in black,

And cannot understand why I, downhearted,
Watch sadly the declining Sunday sun.
'The blower, darling? Lord, 1 haven't started,
'But next week-end perhaps I'll get it done.'

BACK SEAT RIDE

Lean back and watch the treetops whirling eastward,
The smoke of stars curls up the Milky Way;
Beyond the silhouetted hills dark purple
There lingers still some limpid field of day.

The tailpipe thrums its throaty diapason
From gear to gear and siraight-cut axle sings,
Our backwash ripples down the supine grasses,
Creation dozes, we alone have wings.

And night is charged with fragrance born of sunshine,
Stored up within the hawthorn and the pine;
Even the tang of oil, like alien incense,
Lifts up with bean and lilac to combine.

Archaic Zeiss reflectors split the shadows
In midnight-blue and bottle-green, to mark
Familiar trees with limbs of primal monsters,
Then fling them down the avenues of dark.

The drub of tyres on tarmac's changing texture,
The blattering wind on eyelids lax with sleep
Hark back in some mysterious way to childhood
When night held all of magic in her keep,

And music of the worn slap-happy pistons,
The engine note, deep-gobbling and sublime,
Become the echoes of some charmed existence
Beyond the stars and out of reach of time.

VINTAGE OMAR

Come, lead me to the Pool at four and three,
I still can give eleven m.p.g.,
All Roads must end before the selfsame Pub,
And Closing Time awaits for Thee and Me.

Oh, be not one with those Tea-drinking men
Who wait until the Tax is twelve pounds ten,
To run their Vintage Motorcars in June,
Then wrap them up in Cotton-wool again.

Myself when young did love to take the Mike
Out of old Motors whom I did not like,
Enquiring how Boanerges was sprung
And if forgotten Caesar rode a Bike.

But mourn me not, whose Day is all but done;
My Wheels, Pumps, Mags and Shockers, one by one,
Shall nurture needy Brothers of the Marque:
No Car may end, that was so well begun.

And Thou, who dost with Bitter and with Gin
Confound the Car Park we manoeuvre in,
Amongst these modern Motors have a care;
My Rump is mighty still, their Wings are Tin.

My Crankshaft Crystals tremble on the Brink,
Tomorrow brings the Breaker's Yard I think,
And gives Thee thy new Jaguar—TO-DAY
Defies Disaster and deludes with Drink.

The Lights will change, no matter who dissents;
Drink up, and do not wait upon Events:
High Octane still must perish in the Pipe,
And costly Vintage vanish in the Gents.

I sometimes think that never goes the Car
So swiftly as when Fumes of Castrol R
Have charmed the Nose all afternoon and then
Give place to double Brandies in the Bar.

So should Thyself, who oftentimes hast got
One up on those who thought they knew the Lot,
Meet with some Type who shoots a lousier Line
Than once did we, then crown him with a Pot.

Ah, Bend of my Delight that needs no Brake,
Where he who rounds the Bend to Grass must take;
How oft hereafter Independent Squeal
Shall keep the angry Residents awake.

And when thy sleek XK is in the Van
On Roads where I was but an Also-ran,
At Opening Time, pause by the Pumps, and where
I once drank deep, fill up thy Jerrican.

ICHABOD

At last the filthy thing is done,
So by the fire we sit
And talk about our future plans,
And never speak of It.

There's a baby in the Carry-cot,
Another on the stocks,
There are bills upon the mantelpiece
And me upon the rocks.

So now we shall not share with her
The roads of home again;
He is coming to collect her
On the early morning train.

The ally of her engine glows,
Her paintwork shines a mile;
When from these loving hands she goes,
By God, she goes in style.

I've left the One-make badge in place,
He says he'll join the Club,
But I rather hope he doesn't
Lest we meet him in our pub.

Maybe we're sentimental fools
But too much pain we'd feel
To see that pair of clueless hands
On our familiar wheel.

I've taken off the foglamp
And hidden it away,
To grace another classic front
Another distant day.

But it won't mean a lot by then
How prosperous we are,
For it's not by spending money
That you get to love a car.

Next week we'll have recovered
From this small domestic stir,
But to-night beside the fire we sit
And do not speak of Her.

IMPOSTHUMOUS MOTORS UNLTD.

or Here We Go Gathering Mutts in May

You'n me 'ad best get cracking, Bert,
The papers ses it's spring,
The bint is in the 'igh Street
And the boyo want's 'is fling.

So up wiv them tarpaulings
We whipped orf Wotsisname,
And shove the Riley near the fence
To 'ide its busted frame.

And where there's orl that grease and muck
We'll put the pore ole Leaf,
So's nosey parkers cannot 'ave
A butcher's underneaf.

Just slosh arahnd an oily rag
On some of that there rust,
And fix this big rev-counter on,
Don't matter if it's bust.

Get Ernie on the blower
And see if 'e can find
A five gal drum of ally paint
'is mates 'ave left be'ind.

We'll want it for this ruddy lot,
And if there's any left,
Be sure tell Ernie put it back.
(I never 'eld wiv theft).

Nah, 'ere's the Wolsey 'ornet
Jim scarpered wiv in Brum,
And the Ford young Alfie borrered
From 'is bird's 'arf dopey chum,

And from a Pompey car park
The 'illman Minx I fahnd;
Cor strike me purple, Bertie boy,
'ow we do get arahnd.

Get weaving with the Vox'all
Wot put a conrod through,
And use a drop of melted lead
If plarsticene won't do,

And mark it up 'Two 'undred nicker,
'Needing slight repare,'
A bloke can't keep in business, Bert,
Unless 'e's more than fair.

But you an me is 'onest men,
Not lahsy lah-di-dahs
Like them bleeders in the 'igh Street,
Miraculous ruddy Cars.

THE MEN WHO WENT TO BRIGHTON

When benzole mix. was one and six,
The Thirty Ninety-Eight
Southward on summer evenings
Would violently migrate.

The Brighton Road at nine o'clock,
The lukewarm sea by ten,
Hot sandwiches in Sandy's Bar
And back to Town again,

Hoping the cops of Croydon
By then were well abed;
The cost for four large gentlemen
Was three and six a head.

But now the stuff is four and three
And next year may be five,
The men who went to Brighton
Must be content to dive

In tame and tepid local baths,
And afterwards to roam,
On beastly little two-strokes,
Suburban roads of home.

For now but two things go untaxed
Which give you any fun,
(Though the men who went to Brighton
Only can think of one),

And not so much for tanks and ships
Go out those precious bobs,
But for busy little bureaucrats
In busy little jobs.

For mingy little minutes
To make their files complete,
For shiny little motorcars,
Where others use their feet.

But, puttering on their two-strokes
About those English lanes,
Where other little bureaucrats
Put field and tree in chains,

The men who went to Brighton,
With anger in their eyes,
Dream of a distant day to be
When all like they shall rise,

When the motorists of England
Shall drive with horrid glee
Ten thousand little bureaucrats
In convoy to the sea,

And push them off the Palace Pier,
And once again be free.

THE ENTHUSIAST

One man I knew put all of us to shame,
He drove the last decrepitude of cars
And vilely drove, his head among the stars,
Bemused with wistful dreams he could not name.
For just one year the too-devoted flame
Against all sense and nature in him burned,
Then, penniless, with riddled lungs, returned
Him to the sanatorium whence he came.

To him it all was paradise come true;
Down empty roads he knew the vestal light
Of daybreak after driving through the night,
And slumbrous crimson winter dusk he knew,
Small pubs on moorland heights, the patient queue
For Silverstone, the wilderness of rain:
All this he tasted once and not again,
For whom life smiled awhile and then withdrew.

But we, who shared with him that halcyon year
And pulled his leg because he drove so badly,
Remember how he took to laughter gladly
And gave no sign at all and showed no fear.
If he is wakeful yet, then may the dear
And tuneless music of that engine note,
Which charmed him so, into his silence float,
And all his happy miles again be near.

And if he sleeps, then somewhere may he wake
And find a wheel to hold, a road to take.

BROOKLANDS MEMORIAL—GOODWOOD

When the last man is gone who still recalls
The steep Home Banking baking in the sun,
Where once the sleek and treadless Dunlops spun
Their circling web of legend on its walls,
Here, in the babel of the Paddock stalls,
This relic of old battles lost and won
By men long dead and cars whose day is done,
Outlasts Time's chequered bunting as it falls.

And it may be, as changing custom passes,
St. Mary's dip shall echo all day long
None save the rooks' and tractor's rusty song,
And Woodcote sleep again beneath its grasses,
And but one precious shard of concrete store
The print of drifting wheels for evermore.

RALLYE GROTESQUE

Your start control the Withered Arms, St.
        Septic-in-the-Sewer,
Your time past midnight on Walpurgis Eve;
The line of grim and groaning cars in front grows ever
        fewer,
Then the grisly marshal beckons and you leave.

Your pallid navigator sniffs cocaine in wild alarm
As you press past prison gates and crematorium,
To take the six foot watersplash within the sewage farm,
Then the first control at Regis Vomitorium.

One marshal's in a muck-heap, another down a well,
While a third has hanged himself from yonder tree;
You flounder through the midden as you wonder how to
    tell
Which cadaver signs your road-book of the three.

The secret test then takes you to the dank decaying city,
With the night of torment scarcely yet begun,
To disembowel a member of the Rally Sub-Committee,
And bring to the finish proof of what you've done.

So by Little Tarting on to Upper Binting,
By Bedworthy down to Wallow-in-the-Creek,
Past villages with names too rude for printing
To towns with names too horrible to speak,

Till you reach a blasted airfield where it's fifty-five below,
For your high speed laps before the light of day,
Where cars with even numbers round the circuit clockwise
    go,
While the wretched odds gyrate the other way.

The breakfast stop, Red Biddy and a reefer cigarette;
Then driving tests your failing wits disperse;
Acceleration you are never likely to forget,
Down one in three, blindfolded, in reverse.

And so you stagger homeward, ere your coma overcomes,
Dim, daft, delirious, dopey, dazed and drained,
And that evening in the local, you tell the wondering
    chums
'A quiet trip, it never even rained.'

COUNSEL TO MAIDENS

Oh damsel fair, beware the car
Where seating space is wider far
Than any man of reason needs
Except to further his misdeeds;
The steering-column change eschew,
No good can come of it for you,
And likewise any motor shun
From which you can't bale out and run.

Let maiden modesty decide
To take a summer evening ride
In something of the vintage breed,
For virtue's friend was ever speed.
No vulpine sibilance can come
From guileless lips of vintage chum,
With passion he is never dizzy,
(His motor keeps him far too busy)
And vintage bucket seats preclude
The acrobatic interlude.

Nor can he sit you in the back,
For there a jerrican, a jack,
An inner tube, some oily rags,
A pair of mouldy flannel bags,
A grease gun, several tattered maps,
Dead bottles left by other chaps,
A tow rope and a grimy glove
Leave not a lot of room for love.

Don Juan hands it to his betters
To flirt with triple carburettors,
And modern Casanovas thrive
On ultrahydramatic drive,
But vintage bod of stark appearance
Gives his poppets ample clearance,
He keeps his honour engine-bright,
Is never loose and seldom tight.

And should the half-elliptic ride
Bring bruise to tender underside,
Those precious nylons go to hell
Among the spanners in the well,
And gearbox cast a blob or two
On tiny white and cherished shoe,
These are but little things to pay
For being out of Danger's way,
The while you blind to Kingdom Come
And back again, intact, to Mum.

The trouble is, the vintage brew
At length may prove too strong for you,
And if with him you ride a lot,
You'll end by marrying the clot.

So, all in all, it seems to us
You're safer riding on a bus.

BOYS BARGAIN

Corded wheel and cramping cockpit,
Engine's hard and even beat,
Smells of petrol, fog and autumn,
Driving down Great Portland Street.

Bonnet strap and outside handbrake
Culminating boyhood's dreams;
Sudden fear, as quickly stifled,
Can this be the snip it seems?

For one sweet and breathless moment
One with all the Great who meet,
Bentley, Alfa, Rolls, Bugatti,
Daily down Great Portland Street.

One with Jarrott, Segrave, Birkin,
With the giants that have been,
Glimmer of their bygone glory
Glinting on an aero screen.

All too soon the anticlimax;
Smell of burning rubber, till
Lights begin to fail in Hampstead,
Brakes to bind at Muswell Hill.

Oil gauge zeroes nearing Southgate,
Clutch burns out at Walthamstow,
Spare falls off in Epping Forest,
Timing slips at Chigwell Row.

Ammeter discharging madly,
Wild backfires to shake the skies
Slowly down the long road homeward
Limps the buyer and his prize.

*   *   *

Long ago that disillusion,
Bills all paid, so hard to meet;
Still remains that breathless moment
Driving down Great Portland Street.

KIDDIEKAR KORNER

or Cursory Rhymes for our Tiniest Clots

Step on it, Baby, on the by-pass;
They are down to the rivets and shiny as glass;
When roundabout warns you must slow to a crawl,
Down will come Baby, brake-linings and all.

Little Jack Horner went into his corner
Determined to do it like Stirling;
Three good fairies came to his aid just the same,
Messrs. Al-Fin, Ferodo, and Girling.

Little Jack Homer went out of his corner
Convinced he had done it like Duncan,
But the stewards just frowned at the state of the ground
And a hedge unaccountably shrunken.

Forty m.p.g. on crude,
Kerosene or treacle;
That's the way to dodge the tax,
CLONK goes the Diesel.

Jack and Jill went up the hill,
The tractor's aid renouncing;
Jack took a dive, full fathom five,
Jill just went on bouncing.

Humpty Bumpty was rarin' to go,
Was airborne at Becketts and landed at Stowe;
All the course marshals, press critics and mockers
Couldn't make Humpty unbutton his shockers.

Mary drove her motor pram
With a Three Fifty Bug.
Every time she changed a nappy,
Baby had to change a plug.

Mobile copper catches Whopper
In the Dirty Thirty;
Dame in Whopper, lets him stop her,
Looks distinctly shirty.
Facetious copper, most improper,
Says 'You should race a Cooper.'
Says dame in Whopper 'Clueless copper,
'My husband is the Super.'

Three blind types,
See them have fun:
They've bust all the glasses in both of the bars,
That the pub's not in ruins give thanks to your stars,
Why doesn't Mine Host take a swipe at the cars
Of three blind types?

Ride a forty c.c.
From London to Leigh;
Start yesterday morning, get there after tea,
With lumbago, neuritis
And a cold in the nose,
He still must keep pedalling wherever he goes.

Little boy marshal, come pull out your flags,
There's a Nash in the meadow, the corn's full of Jags.
Where is the one to take care of these chaps?
On top of a haystack, taking snaps.

Mary, Mary, stark and airy,
How did your Bolster go?
Mit Donner und Blitzen, mit Kampf und Einsitzen,
And elbows all in a row.

Here lies a young man in a Rover,
Who diced on the cliff-top at Dover,
Until Lateral g.
Ceased his playmate to be,
And to Vertical g. handed over.

AUTHOR'S ACKNOWLEDGMENTS

Acknowledgments to all who make
Our motoring amusing,
To chaps who write up regs and take
Great pains to be confusing.

To kindergarten racer who
With beerlogged science blinds,
To lovers of the Vintage brew
(If slightly corked, who minds?)

To him who, traffic busting through,
Goes by upon the right,
Then can't get back into the queue
And has to wait all night.

To exhibitionist and drunk,
Kerb-crawler, clown and clot,
To anyone who helps debunk
The whole confounded lot.

And last of all to him who brooks
No hint that here is he,
Yet, as he through these pages looks,
Himself may chance to see.

CLUB HANDICAP—SILVERSTONE

I must have been asleep till now, else why should I have
    done it?
They said 'Your motor is quite fast, you really ought to
    run it';
Now here is Horace Bluebell, and there Hydraulic Sid,
And here am I (oh why, oh why?) upon the starting grid.

The flag goes down and Basil's off in one almighty burst,
I lumber gently in his wake, still poking out of first;
Poor unprotesting propshaft, oh do not fail I pray,
I change to third (it can be heard a hundred miles away).

Now here comes Geoff. and here comes rain in great
    unwieldy drops,
And here come I, spectators sigh, and here, Good Lord,
    comes Copse;
Flag marshal grinning broadly, and tyres are such a price,
And here is rain and here is Geoff. (he must have passed
    me twice).

I envy everybody else, especially the chaps
Who ride round in Mark Sixes and alter handicaps,
The field goes by in sheets of spray (what! Was that
    Geoff. again?)
I'm sitting on a wet wet seat, I hope it's only rain.

My knees are made of rubber and my hands are made of
    butter,
I've bashed my ruddy knuckles, the exhaust begins to
    stutter,
My goggles slide right down my nose and will not stay
    upon it,
While sounds like bells and frightful smells come from
    beneath the bonnet.

And Hangar Straight goes slopping by in one rain-bleary
      blot,
I'm a nitwit, I'm a moron, I'm a coward, I'm a clot,
The rest have all gone home by now or else they're having
      tea.
And Silverstone is empty save for miserable me.

I'd like a double brandy, I'd like to be in bed,
If this goes on much longer, I'd like to be damn dead;
At last the flag, the Paddock, the easing-up of strain,
And packing up the picnic things and bucketsful of rain,

And I would give a hundred quid to have it all again.

LAMENT FOR A LOUSY HANDBOOK

When I rush to my book at the double,
I read with a fury that irks:
'This component will never give trouble;
'If it does, send it back to the Works.'

Not a hint as to how it's adjusted,
No word of what might go amiss,
Nor how I can tell if it's busted,
Nor what I'm to do if it is.

The Works, now just part of a combine,
Discontinued my model at birth;
They make globular motors for export
To impossible parts of the earth.

The designer retired in frustration,
All the drawings they managed to lose;
The Stores have no spares situation
Since the storekeeper went on the booze.

No one left to bring help at the double,
Just the typewritten answer that irks:
'This component will always give trouble;
'We don't want it back here at the Works'

DRIVING TESTS

Right lock, left lock, stop astride the line,
This driver and his motor-car are doing mighty fine;
Wiggle-woggle parking test, round and round and round,
Four and twenty pylons a'lying on the ground.
First, not top, you ruddy clot, now into reverse;
She handles like a tractor converted to a hearse,
Five neutrals in the gearbox, no absorbers in the shock,
Oh where, oh where have my anchors gone, oh where,
      oh where is my lock?
I've bounced across the promenade, I've landed on the
      beach,
Oh lash me to the reeling helm ere it be out of reach;
Spectators' gusty laughter above the ocean's din,
The sands of time are running out, the tide is running in.
Oh throw the towrope hither for me and for my car,
Oh haul me past those gaping crowds, oh haul me fast
      and far
        Where stopwatch threatens never,
        Clutch linings last for ever,
        And the lousiest over-revver
        May stop astride the bar.

THE ROAD TO WINCHESTER

Go down the road to Winchester as steady as a rock,
Rev counter on four thousand and eighty on the clock,
The brazen-throated engine note is singing to the skies
And the little tears whip backward from the corners of
      your eyes.

Turn off the road at Winchester, the rest go swinging
      south;
She has eyes to melt your conscience and a honey of a
      mouth,
There's a picnic in the tonneau and a rug to have it on;
Turn off the road at Winchester before your chance is
      gone.

Come up the road from Winchester as day is growing
      old,
The proud and dusty bonnet thrusting homeward
      through the gold,
With all those cars that kept their heads and took their
      drivers south

And which has won, your conscience or her honey of a
      mouth ?

THE LAY OF THE COMMON DRIVER

The roads were meant for men like me
Since motoring began;
I am the Average Motorist,
I am the Common Man;
And this the substance of my creed,
Culled from experience long;
I have been driving thirty years
And so I can't be wrong.

The left of the road is for learners
And for those who are prone to take fright,
The right of the road is for Frenchmen
And for drunkards adrift in the night,
            So hey diddle diddle
            I'll drive in the middle,
Stop on a blind bend when the wife wants to
            Pick primroses.
I'm a sensible chap and the last who exposes
            A stranger
            To danger,
            I'm no dog in the manger;
            When I drive in the van
            I'm a reasonable man;
Let the fellow behind me get past
            —if he can.

            When I drive in a lane
            Going steeply downhill,
            There is nothing to gain
            Save a possible spill
            If I take to the grass
            Or conceivably stop
            For the misguided ass

Coming up to the top.
I mean no offence
But it's patent to see
If he had any sense
He'd go downhill like me.

Another thing, and this the worst,
When climbing I can't change to first
Because, to irk my weary flesh,
That gear has got no synchromesh;
Why don't the cars descending, pray,
Pull more aside and give me way?

The sports car bears a selfish lout,
The bicycle the same;
If I've left my Trafficator out,
The makers are to blame,
And if across your path I go
Without a warning due,
I have my rights I'd have you know
And the onus is on you.

But as I've often said before,
I'm an open-minded chap;
Cars older than mine are a menace
And all should be broken for scrap,
New cars should go for export
And leave the highway free
For those who best deserve it,
For the Common Men like me.

I guard the middle of the road,
I dip no lamp by night,
I have been driving thirty years
And so I must be right.

C.W. and P.

I had a little axle; it gave me four point five,
The wind sang sweetly past my ears, my motor was alive;
I thought 'This is terrific—I've only one desire—
'I'll go a little quicker if I gear a little higher.'

I have a little axle; it gives me four to one,
My life is spent on second, my motor gets no fun,
And traffic is a torment and climbing hills a pain;
I wish I had my four point five to drive me once again.

THE OLD SIXES

It is believed that many long chassis $6\frac{1}{2}$ litre Bentleys, still
exist in storage. They will never be of much use now for
they are too large for today's traffic conditions and are too
small to convert into flats.

We are ancient, we are cumbrous, limousine or landaulette,
And to mouldering inactivity resigned,
Making homes for mice and spiders but we never quite
forget
All those miles for which our motors were designed.
When enthusiastic misters sought our slinky Speed Six
sisters
In the Thirties, we'd no sex-appeal for men;
With our power too highly rated and our lines so
out-of-dated,
They passed us by and didn't need us then.

Of Bedford cord and solid hide we still are rather vain
Where the rumps of Dukes and Dowagers reclined;
Charles the chauffeur, James the valet out in front and in
the rain,

And two footmen on the luggage grid behind.
When the Home Guard called for motors, they just took
                                                    away our rotors,
Chose the economic Eight or family Ten,
Though for action we were bursting and our gallant
                                                    Smiths were thirsting,
They passed us by and didn't need us then.

Through the length and breadth of Britain, north to
                                                    Scotland west to Wales,
In dark barns or sheds forgotten you will find
The Big Six Bentleys sleeping through a night that never
                                                    pales,
Out of fashion, out of sight and out of mind.
When the war at last had ended we had hoped to be
                                                    befriended,
But they stripped our tops for housing for the hen,
Stealing bits from seven-seaters for those upstart old
                                                    3-litres,
They passed us by and didn't need us then.

Though Bentleys with four paltry pots the limelight now
                                                    have got,
Time comes for them, no matter how refined,
When with their fun and games the B.D.C. use up the lot,
Time comes when hubs no more can be resplined.
When crankshaft crystals crumble, dying sun-and-planets
                                                    rumble
To cacophanous decrepitude, and when
The Old School's whole existence rests upon our glued-up
                                                    pistons
Will they seek us out and will they need us then?
Will they take us, treat us well, will they love us?
                                                    Will they hell!
With our cathedraic coachwork after Wren;

When each fickle heart rejoices in those Bentleys—
                              like Rolls-Royces,
They'll pass us by and will not need us then.

THE CONTINENTAL BOYS

We are the Continental Boys,
We have the guts and nerve
To sample all of Europe's joys
In one Majeure Epreuve.

We do three thousand in a week,
We are the distance beaters—
Of course, of miles we never speak
But always kilometres.

We drink the wine, we eat the food,
We have the indigestion,
But if it does us any good
Is quite another question.

Our tanks and radiators gain
Unnatural deposits,
With us the memories remain
Of dreadful water-closets.

Through punctures, when no spare avails,
In Alps and Pyrenees,
We've broken all our finger nails
And worn away our knees.

Stan says that he had never known
France held so many clots,
Now Jack has got a gasket blown
And Jill come out in spots.

While Bill is not on speaking terms
With Tom who has lumbago;
We fear poor Harry has had worms
And June an affair with a dago.

Our split lips bear a poisoned look,
We are a lot of wrecks;
Now Sam has lost his pocket-book
With all his Autocheques.

We are the Continental Boys;
Browned off? No, that's sunburn,
But sweetest of all Europe's joys
Awaits when we return

And tell old George who stayed in Kent
And Geoff. who toured in Devon,
How half across the world we went
And how it all was heaven.

MIRACULOUS MOTORS LTD.

Miraculous Motors and Gorgeous Cars
Are the envy of all in the Trade
And the topic for salesmen who prop up the bars
In the places where bargains are made.

They've M.G.'s by the score and Lagondas galore
And Bentleys both early and late,
Of Bugattis all main types, Invictas with drainpipes
—Or so their advertisements state.

'To see is to try and to try is to buy',
Such snips so they say can be met there;

If you rush there next morning, take heed of this warning,
All these cars will be sold when you get there.

You will find an old shed where rain leaks on your head,
And a Special more dead than alive,
An indigent Twenty with sorrows a'plenty
(They call it a fine Twenty-Five).

There's an engineless Mouse at the back of the house,
Half a jeep and a bicycle frame,
And that, chum, is the lot that these merchants have got;
Now hear their 'director' declaim:

'A Colonel R.E. bought the Blower M.G.
'And a Groupie the Bug—what a car—
'We've just sold the 8-litre to dear old Sir Peter
'And the Rolls to a radio star.'

'We've a Trojan due in and it motors like sin
'But that Special—you cannot go wrong;
'Just you try her, old boy, she's a positive joy
'At eight hundred no more than a song.'

As you leave, render thanks that these titles and ranks
All your efforts to buy can forestall,
For the car in the picture, undeserving of stricture,
May have never existed at all.

Miraculous Motors and Gorgeous Cars
By some are regarded as cads,
But how great is our pleasure in reading at leisure
Miraculous Gorgeous Ads.

DIVINE AROMA

So Castrol R is back in pungent glory,
Nostalgic, oleaginous and sweet,
And half an hour at Boreham or at Goodwood
Shall set your jaded nose upon its feet.

It's twin-cylinder G.N.'s and belt-drive Nortons,
It is Brooklands on Bank Holiday as well,
And mucking up a perfectly good engine
Just to get the golden glory of the Smell.

The savour of burnt almonds is perfection
Now wedded to a castor base at last,
The thin blue haze makes mirage in the sunshine
To conjure up the paddocks of the past.

And when you point your bonnet to Valhalla
To learn anew the old enthralling game,
As you change up just beyond the Spiral Nebulae,
What else is strange, the Smell will be the same.

O.P.

'Oil pressure at two thousand, hot, is forty pounds or so,
'And if it is not forty pounds, your motor will not go.'
Thus spake the learned makers in their clever little book,
And so, at that small instrument, I seldom dare to look.

Sometimes on biting winter morn, when bitter frost abides,
The needle crawls to shaky ten, then sleepily subsides;
Oh clueless clot though I may be, is not this car a hero,
Have we not gone ten thousand miles, oil pressure, hot,
        at zero?

SPECIAL

Engine by Riley,
Extensively rebored,
Suspension (front) by Fiat,
Suspension (rear) by Ford.

Body by A. N. Onymous,
Rather tired and tatty,
Accessories by Breaker's Yard,
Colour by Bugatti.

Instruments by Air Ministry,
Tuning by Mister Clever,
Braking by the Grace of God,
Tyres by Never Never.

Tribulations by the thousand,
Rare triumphs one by one,
Faith and Hope and Charity
By the blooming ton

SPRING SONG

Sing hey ninny nonnet and up with the bonnet
Once more of my four and a half,
With bearings past praying and drain-tubes decaying,
If the sun shone I woodenarflarf.

While others go courting, I track down the shorting
Between dynamo, cutout and switch;
No one else's drop-arm ever causes alarm
Whereas mine lands me bang in the ditch.

The header-tank leaks, I've a brake-drum that shrieks,
The pump and the water-plates ooze,
I've no date with a popsy, the sump's full of dropsy
And I've gear-oil all over my shoes.

My funny-bone's numb and I've busted my thumb,
I've cracked glass in my windscreen and lamps,
The rev-counter's gone sour and gives miles per hour,
While the oil gauge is reading in amps.

Let other blokes chatter at Noggin and Natter,
Admiring the motors they drive,
Under floorboards I squirm like an oversize worm
And am lucky to come out alive.

A chap didn't oughter flaunt four and a quarter
Fat litres of polish and pelf,
And smoke a cigar while he props up the bar
When I barely can prop up myself.

Sing hey for the springtime, for new piston-ring time,
'D' boxes and poppets and fun;
While you flirt with the breeze, I'll be down on my knees
With a five twenty-five twenty-one.

VINTAGE REUNION

Dear heaven, I would know you anywhere,
That battered Weymann grandeur, like an old
Decrepit actor's cloak which needs enfold
So much of secret shameful wear and tear;
An actor with a faint piratic air
Who, on the changing stages of the roads,
Plays all his parts and carries all his loads,
And dreams he hears applause no longer there.

Now children picnic on your running boards:
Do you, as I, remember all that's been,
Our walk-on part in Wearing of the Green,
Our towsing of the Packards and the Fords?

And now I can but watch you from the stalls
And wish you well until your curtain falls.

DEHYDRATED DICING

Time was when chaps tried out a car by going on the road
And a stopwatch told the total that they got,
Then they'd find a sharpish corner, put the motor under
load
And some would get around and some would not.

But now you draw yourself a pint and settle at your case
For by mathematics all the work is done,
With seven-figure logarithms, a brace of B.Sc's,
A slide-rule and some paper for your fun.

Take the litres ton-mile dry, between limits integrate
That the licensing authorities may choose,
Multiply by piston area, add the cube root of the date,
And divide by Laurence Pomeroy's size in shoes.

Then raise it to the power of the tangent of slip angle,
Unless of course your chassis oversteers,
When the differential calculus will quickly disentangle
Your first equation till it disappears,

When you plot a set of curves showing coefficient's drag,
And project the frontal area till it meets,
And there the answer is before you, absolutely in the bag,
To tell you where to put your paper sheets.

So now there is no longer need to test our heroes' nerves
In racing with its sorrows and its joys
When everything from club events to leading Grandes
Epreuves
Can be done by telephone and back-room boys.

Imagine the excitement when the chief Ferrari crack
Makes an error in subtraction on the line,
And when Alfa's two-stage slide-rule catches fire down the
      back,
And the B.R.M. wins out by half a sine.

RUDYARD BENTLING

Or what a great poet might have made of a great Marque

She's a poor old green jalopy, all her piston rings are
      sloppy,
And her pitted bearings tote a wicked load,
Her paintwork's lost its shine but she's doubly, trebly
      mine
By the laws that rule the kinship of the Road.

There is music in the beat of her thrumming, drumming
      feet,
Old in years but in her spirit ever young;
How she'd cock her blunted nose, grumble 'Brother,
      here I goes'
And battle past the sleek and softly sprung.

She will lavish all her love on the hand in velvet glove
Upon the gears that give the glory to the Game,
But she'll make her anger heard if you muff your change
      to third
And she'll send you packing, beetroot-faced with shame.

Let them talk of turbine cars and of rockets to the stars
In the places where men worship the Machine,
But one loyal grimy crew will push back your teeth for you
If you dare insult the grand old girl in green.

She's a poor old green jalopy, all her wings are cracked
    and floppy,
And she's sadly near the ending of her span,
But what modern car dare laugh at her simple epitaph
'Ever faithful to her Task and to her Man'?

VINTAGE BROTHERHOOD

We are the Vintage brotherhood, our cars are very old,
Each thing sits in its proper place and we sit in the cold,
Conducting our machinery behind an aero screen,
While little boys cry 'Racer' and the moderns wax obscene.

Our cars may make more noise than theirs, they may not
    go as fast,
They've no push-button radio, but heavens how they last;
These then our loved and trusted friends, of more than
    human worth,
For craftsmanship and character, the greatest things on
    earth.

The Aston is a gentleman, this no one will deny,
His copious oil is ever cool, his well-cut gears are high;
He shares, with lean Lagonda, that secret of the past,
Of how to wear a cycle wing, and how to make it last.

The Bentley is a jovial chap, his lines are sleek and
    pleasant,
He trumpets gaily down the roads, a two-ton adolescent;
But when at rest, his water-pump weeps hot nostalgic
    tears,
Remembering the glories of those green and bygone years.

The Talbot's an eccentric type, tied up in metric thread,
You take her body off before you can detach her head,
And if you wish to drop the sump, rear axle first remove;
Oh, how the Talboteers must work if they would gain her
        love.

Patrician Thirty Ninety-Eight, all lesser types atop,
No doubt because he's never known just how and when to
        stop,
The sane and simple Alvis, with a rabbit on the rad,
The Austin Seven ever making modern motors mad.

The Merc. with outside plumbing like the Corporation
        drains,
The Frazer Nash who strews our roads with little bits of
        chains,
Old Bullnose and Two Lunger, those maids of work for all,
The Riley, Leaf and Lambda—their charms shall never
        pall.

We are the Vintage brotherhood, our cars are hell to run,
The moderns get the spares they need, but we get all the
        fun,
No hydromatic nonsense, no bulbous tin for us—

And if you break a crankshaft, you can always take a bus.

DICER

One evening in a traffic jam through rain I strove to see,
And eased past motor bus and van my hundred B.H.P.
When swiftly past my vision swam a one two five c.c.

A dignified old gentleman on this frail carriage sat,
He did not wear an overcoat, he did not wear a hat,
But wove among the traffic lanes as hell emits a bat.

Correcting slides on greasy setts with cunning cant and
    swerve,
He vanished out of sight around a wrongly-cambered
    curve;
He had the legs of all of us and he had all the nerve.

This elderly virtuoso, alas, in vain I've sought,
Perhaps he only does his stuff in rain and traffic caught,
Or has done it once too often and a final Burton bought

Men have made gods of dicing types since dicing first
    began,
Of Fangio or Farina you may be an ardent fan,
But ever I'll give pride of place to an unknown bald old
    man.

NONSENSE RHYME

Take any impotent barouche and paint it vivid yellow,
Print a motto on the bonnet to show you're quite a fellow,
Add phoney racing numbers in white on discs of black
And the Fishtail to end all fishtails on the plumbing at the
      back;
Then polish all the shiny parts and any bits that aint
Load down with thick and slobbery coats of aluminium
      paint;
Pose a popsy on the scuttle of this monarch of machines,
Dressed neatly in a stoneguard and a pair of aero screens,
Then get photographed in crash-hat beside the whole
      contraption,
Send to any Sunday paper complete with silly caption
'Major Squat the racing motorist, Miss Squit the rising
      star',
And then go home and hang yourself and burn your
      ruddy car.

S.T.D.

Beards and funny shirts and wheelspin,
Tide of sound that ebbs and flows,
And another Brighton Speed Trials
Ambles to its noisy close.

Exquisite girls with oil-black fingers,
Alfa red, Bugatti blue,
Bentley green and horrid hybrid,
Nightmare bedstead Special too.

Hear the tireless commentator
Reeling off the times and knots;
Homage for the practised masters,
Caustic comment for the clots.

Now the inquests are beginning,
And inverted lineshoots pall;
Somewhere in this roaring Bedlam
Stands the Slowest Car of All.

Weeks of urgent work and worry,
Press on Regardless, Do or Die,
Ending up in fuel starvation,
Plugs too hard or gears too high.

When you burble gently homeward,
As September shadows fall,
Spare a thought, if but in passing,
For that Slowest Car of All.

YEHUDI BROS.

Yehudi Brothers are two men
Of very small dimensions;
They work like blazes now and then,
They have the best intentions.

Once they were gremlins, so they say,
Then came to see the light;
They roost within my car by day
And do their stuff by night.

One leaps ahead and switches on
The cats' eyes down the road,
One waits behind till I have gone,
Then quickly sheds the load.

If Number One should go astray,
I know what I must do:
Fit fuse or lamp without delay,
But what of Number Two?

If he should fail, poor little chap,
Those sinuous lines of light
Would blazon England's highway map
Beneath the vaulted night.

And lovers on the grass in hordes,
And prowling cats and rabbits
Would query the Electric Board's
Uneconomic habits.

Till such a nation-wide to-do
Might oust the Government;
And all because Yehudi Two
Down the wrong turning went.

TAILPIECE

When you let your car get dirty,
The sun shines hot and long;
If you wash it well then it rains like hell,
So whatever you do, you're wrong.

If you spend a little fortune
Obtaining those extra knots,
The loss in power and miles per hour
Brands you as one of the clots.

But cane your motor with malice
Till it sounds like a load of tins;
It will serve you true and astonish you
One day when it ups and wins.

The moral of all this nonsense,
If you want to have your fun,
Is to do the least to the wretched beast,
And the rest leave well undone.

RAKE'S PROGRESS

When I was but a lawless lad
I thought the highway rules
Were only meant for such as Dad
And other harmless fools.

I took my silencer away,
Without front wings I'd run,
And came to court each month to pay
For all my bits of fun.

Then later I knew other sins
As down the roads I sped,
I bumped a policeman on the shins,
I crossed upon the red.

Was charged with driving while asleep,
And uninsured, and how,
Because I hit a flock of sheep
And somehow killed a cow.

But soon shall I be written down
As the supreme transgressor,
For failing to spend half-a-crown
Upon a small suppressor.

THE OLD CAR—FIRLE HILL CLIMB

Oh the sunshine and the roaring and the story
Of unimportant things superbly done,
The colour and the Castrol and the glory,
The bumps across the paddock and the fun.

The road winds dark against the bleaching grasses,
The last bend wheels into an arc of sky,
As each inexorable second passes
Athwart the shabby Titan that is I.

Gently the flag falls, quicker than we reckoned,
The wheelspin blackens from unsteady heels,
Revs rise up shrieking, blip abrupt to second,
The first bend whistles wildly at our wheels.

The wrench, the slide, and somehow we have made it
The long straight lifts against the blinding blue;
Three thousand, three two hundred, I'm afraid it
Is all this ageing heart is equal to.

The last bend looms above us, rear wheels judder
Across the gritty tarmac in the sun,
Archaic half-elliptics weave and shudder-
It was a lousy climb, but it was fun.

Tormented metal tinkles into quiet,
A lone voice calls 'Not bad, old boy, not bad'
Across the downs the harsh loudspeakers riot
'So far that is the slowest time we've had.'

Now am I old and none is left to fear me,
So ere I shame my Marque, my sister cars,
Maybe a kindly God will scrutineer me
And point this palsied bonnet to the stars.

CLOT

In all my life I have not missed
What any motoring journalist
Has had to say on What to Do
For those who are without a clue,
Devoured all the weightier tomes
Enthusiasts keep in their homes,
And reaped the harvest of the Brains,
Bolster on Specials, also Chains,
Davis on Corners, Pom on Piston Area,
Grown ever wiser, also ever warier;
Studied the Masters, sought to sift
The subtle secret of the Drift;
Those terrible twins, the brothers Steer,
Have been to me as mud made clear,
(Though even now I pause to wonder,
Which is Over, which is Under?),
Read race reports of all the clubs
And the pungent and pertinent Boddy and Tubbs,
Till now such knowledge I have got,
I ought by rights to Know the Lot,
And, if I didn't go so slowly,
Remove the pants from Fagioli.
But still each time away I go,
Forgetting all I didn't know,
Too late or early with my braking,
Blue flags waving, fists a'shaking,
Revolving round those bales of hay,
Getting in everyone else's way,
Sometimes even getting in my own,
The Clot complete, unique, alone.

THE PASSING OF THE BENTLEYS

(Written in 1947 when I feared, happily without foundation, that these noble cars might pass from our ken forever)

Now are they gone, nor ever to return,
The vintage Bentleys that we loved of old,
No more the lean green buccaneers shall burn
The long road westward through a dusk of gold.

No more the convoy, roaring down the night,
Shall shake the proletarian in his sleep,
Nor brave P. Hundreds whip their blinding white
Down roads deserted, into shadows deep.

Romantic? Yes. Utilitarian? No.
They spoilt the Brave New Face of England, chum,
Crowded the parks where Workers' coaches go,
Defiled the lanes where tourist Packards come.

So are they gone, and none to mourn their end,
Save Bentley types in pubs, whose beery sighs
Breathe requiem for each beloved friend,
With whose departure one more Freedom dies.